Bernadette Cuxart

RICHMOND HILL
PUBLIC LIBRARY

JUL 23 2015

CENTRAL LIBRARY
905-884-9288

ART
Stamping

BOOK SOLD
NO LONGER R.H.P.L.
PROPERTY

BARRON'S

eNTS

A GARDEN
with bottles and bubble wrap

We are surrounded by materials that can be very useful for stamping as you'll see in this book!

MATERIALS: Several different bottles, bubble wrap, paints, paintbrushes, card, plates, and a sponge.

1 We're going to make a garden of flowers. To start, pour the paint colors you want to use onto a plate. Using a paintbrush or a sponge, dab globs of colors onto the bubble wrap.

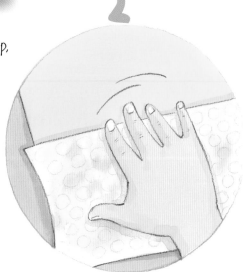

2 Turn it over immediately and stamp it onto the bottom of the card. Press with the palm of your hand so that there are lots of little colored flowers.

3 For larger flowers, paint the bottom of a bottle.

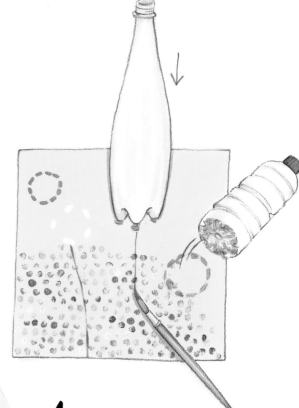

4 Stamp them on the card again, without waiting for the paint to dry. Paint the stalks of the flowers with a paintbrush.

Look for several bottles and check that not all the bottoms are the same size. Take advantage of these differences for your stamping.

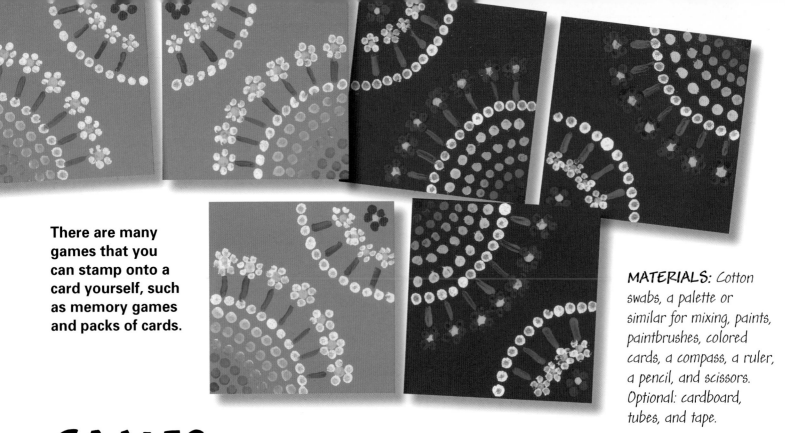

There are many games that you can stamp onto a card yourself, such as memory games and packs of cards.

MATERIALS: Cotton swabs, a palette or similar for mixing, paints, paintbrushes, colored cards, a compass, a ruler, a pencil, and scissors. Optional: cardboard, tubes, and tape.

GAMES with cotton swabs

1

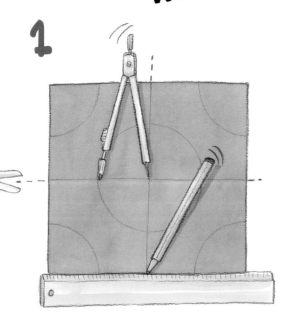

1 Cut out a $7^7/_8$ x $7^7/_8$ in. (20 x 20 cm) square. Divide the square into four equal squares using a pencil. Then draw a circle with a 2 in. (5 cm) radius in the middle. Using the same radius, draw a semicircle in each corner. To finish, cut out the 4 squares.

2

2 Prepare the paints you are going to use and mix the colors. Dip a cotton swab into one color.

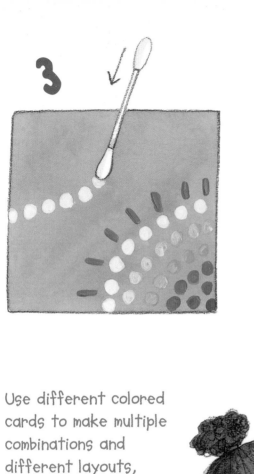

3 Start stamping small circles, following the lines made with the pencil. Decide on a pattern and repeat it.

4 Cotton swabs have a lot of possibilities: by placing them flat, you can make stalks. If you drag them, yo'll get lines. Also try taping some cotton swabs around a tube or in a row on a piece of cardboard.

Use different colored cards to make multiple combinations and different layouts, just by turning the cards. Play around!

HEARTS
and backgrounds with erasers

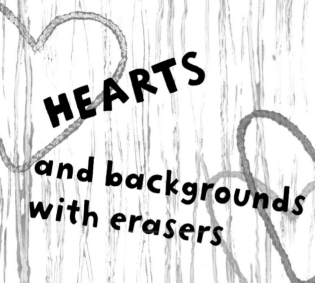

You can make some very original backgrounds with rubber bands. And string is very useful for making figures. Try it out!

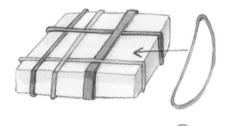

MATERIALS: Rubber bands, string, card, glue, a solid plastic box or wood block, a cardboard tube, cylinder or stick, paints, paintbrushes, a plastic paint tray, card, paper, and scissors.

1

1 Draw a simple shape with glue onto the card. Stick a piece of string onto the glue and cut off the extra. Let it dry for at least two hours.

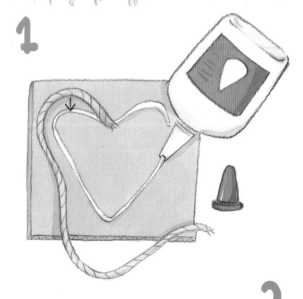

2

2 Place some interwoven elastic bands around the box, as flat as possible. Also place some elastic bands around the tube, slightly separated.

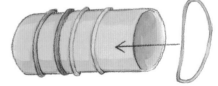

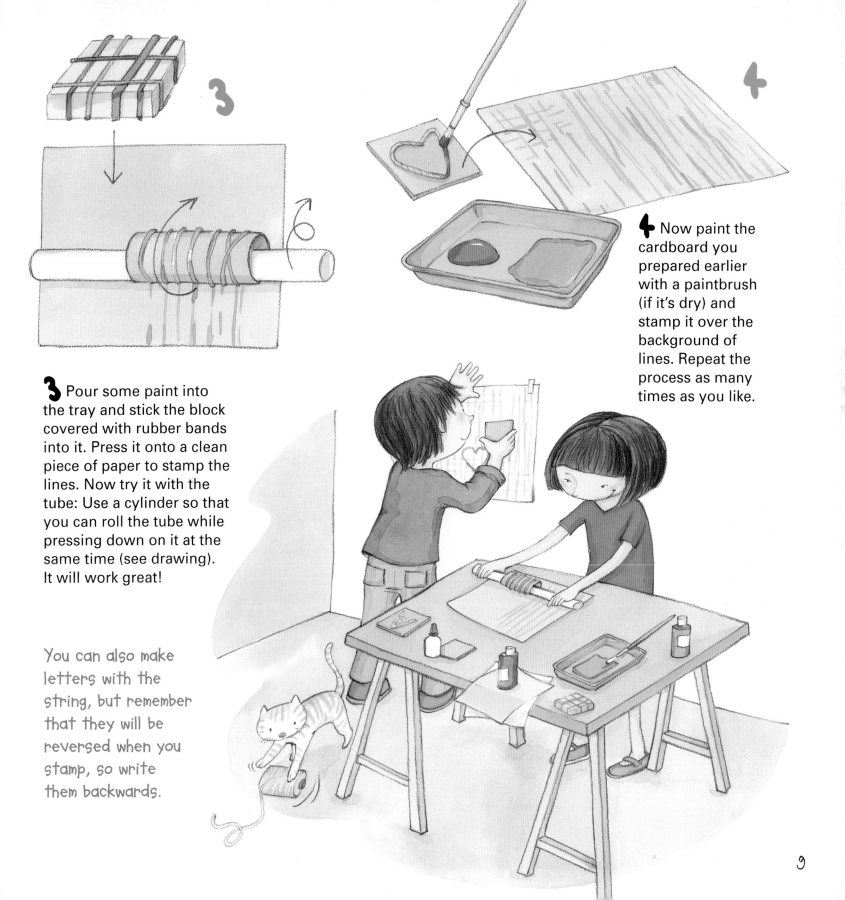

3 Pour some paint into the tray and stick the block covered with rubber bands into it. Press it onto a clean piece of paper to stamp the lines. Now try it with the tube: Use a cylinder so that you can roll the tube while pressing down on it at the same time (see drawing). It will work great!

You can also make letters with the string, but remember that they will be reversed when you stamp, so write them backwards.

4 Now paint the cardboard you prepared earlier with a paintbrush (if it's dry) and stamp it over the background of lines. Repeat the process as many times as you like.

Painting with a sponge is really fun! Because the paint doesn't cover everything, you can see the background color through it. Have you ever done this?

THE SKY
with sponges

MATERIALS:
A bath sponge, different shaped sponges or make-up removers, paints, a tray for mixing, cardboard, scissors, and a pencil.

1

1 Draw a simple shape on a piece of card. Cut out the figure from the inside to "empty" it.

2

2 Now place the shape on another piece of card, using it like a stencil. Hold onto it with one hand so it doesn't move. Take the sponge with your free hand and dip it into the paint. Apply it by dabbing, but not rubbing it over the card, making sure you concentrate on the edges of your stencil. When you think it's ready, remove the stencil carefully.

3 If you have different shaped sponges, you can use them. Otherwise, you can make them by cutting up a large make-up sponge. Make simple figures like those shown in the drawing, for example.

4 Pick the paint you want to use, pour a small amount into a tray and, you're ready to go! Before stamping your project, try out the different possible combinations with the shapes you have. To finish, make the birds' legs and small details with pens.

Before using the sponge for stamping, make sure that nobody in your family is going to need it when they take a shower...

Stamping with your hands or feet always creates a unique result. There are no two identical prints in the world!

MATERIALS:
Your feet or those of a friend, black card, white card, scissors, a polystyrene tray, a sponge, glue, and a hole punch.

GHOSTS with your feet

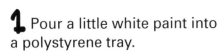

1 Pour a little white paint into a polystyrene tray.

2 Wet a sponge and paint the bottom of your foot (or a friend's).

12

3 Immediately place your foot on the black card, pressing down hard without moving it. Clean the paint off the foot and then repeat with the other one.

4 Now you only have to give your ghosts eyes and a mouth. Did you like it? Try using different colored paints and cards.

To make the circles for the eyes, you can use a hole punch; it's much easier than cutting them out with scissors.

Outdoors, you can find lots of things that you can use for stamping. Leaves are a good example.

LANDSCAPES with leaves

MATERIALS: Different shaped leaves, paints and paintbrushes, a plate, and old newspapers.

1 Collect leaves with different shapes and sizes. Clean them a little if they are dirty, being careful not to break them.

2 Prepare a plate with different colors of paint. Think about the colors of the trees in the fall: greens, yellows, oranges, browns, and reds…

3 Now paint the backs of the leaves, on the side where the veins stand out more. Work on newspaper to avoid marking anything.

4 Stamp onto a sheet of paper, pressing lightly with your hand. Do it one leaf at a time: Paint and stamp, changing colors.

If you put them next to each other, they will look like a forest in the fall. But you can also do other things... What can you think of?

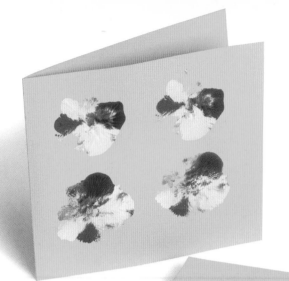

CARNATIONS
with balloons

MATERIALS: Balloons, water, a tray, paints, sheets of paper and/or card, and a green marker (optional).

What do you think of these carnations? You wouldn't be able to obtain these effects with a paintbrush, but with a balloon you can!

1 Pour a little water into the balloon, less than half.

2 Then blow up the balloon a little and tie a knot in it.

16

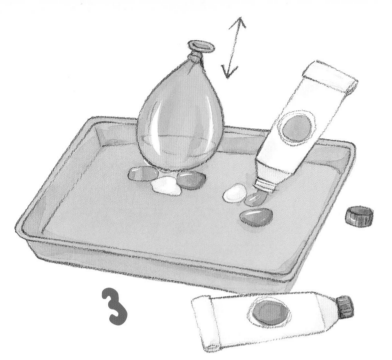

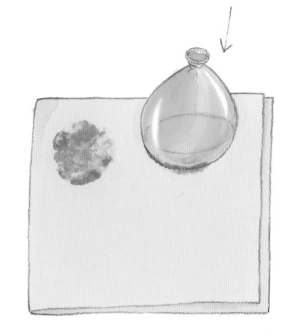

3 Prepare the paints in a tray: squeeze a few drops of different colors to create a circle, like flower petals. Wet a balloon by pressing it right into the middle of the circle.

4 And without wasting any time, press the balloon onto a sheet of paper. It looks like a flower, doesn't it? Also try turning the balloon slightly as you press and see how you make a different type of flower.

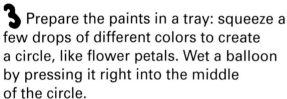

You can finish your flowers by drawing the stalks with a green marker. You can make beautiful greeting cards using this technique!

17

SCENES
with erasers and markers

MATERIALS: Large erasers, felt-tip pens, paper, a pencil, and a paper napkin.

You always have some erasers and markers at home, so you're almost ready to get started stamping.

1 Think about what you want to make. First practice on a sheet of paper, because you won't be able to erase the marker later.

2 When you've decided, draw straight onto the eraser with the markers. Remember that if you make letters, you'll have to write them backwards.

3 Turn the eraser over quickly and press it onto a sheet of paper.
You can use more than one color for each drawing, but don't wait too long, so that the ink doesn't dry...

4 Clean the eraser well after each stamping session using a paper napkin or a cloth.

Another way of cleaning the eraser is to stamp on a different sheet of paper several times until there is no ink left.

A CASTLE

with construction blocks

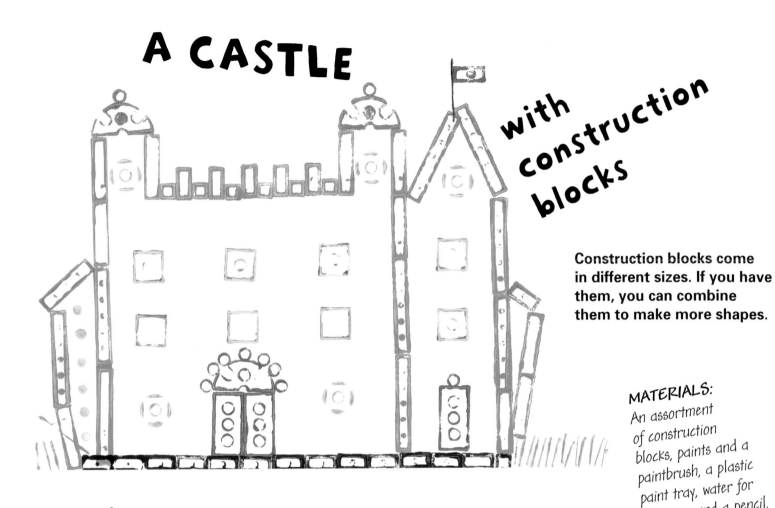

Construction blocks come in different sizes. If you have them, you can combine them to make more shapes.

MATERIALS:
An assortment of construction blocks, paints and a paintbrush, a plastic paint tray, water for cleaning, and a pencil.

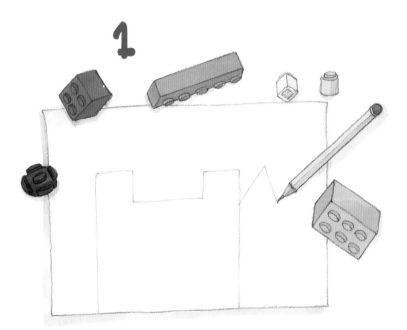

1 Think about what you feel like creating and draw it on a sheet of paper. Then join different pieces together.

2 Using a paintbrush, spread the paint colors you need over a plastic paint tray.

20

3 Take a construction block and make sure the bottom is totally covered with paint by turning it in the tray. Have a piece of paper on hand to test it and remove some of the paint before stamping it onto your drawing.

Remember to clean the pieces every time you change color.

4 Change the pieces and colors however you like, following the drawing you sketched. Notice how you get different figures with one block, depending on which part of it you use.

BORDERS
with a pencil eraser

As well as making borders, you can use the pencil eraser for filling in drawings with little colored circles. You'll love it!

MATERIALS: A pencil with an eraser, paper, and different colored inkpads. If you don't have any inkpads, use a make-up sponge, colored paints, scissors, a cloth, and water for cleaning.

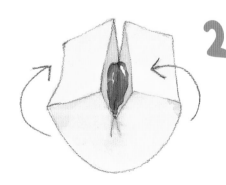

1 Cut the make-up sponge into 1¼ x 1¼ in. (3 x 3 cm) squares and pour a little paint onto each one. You can prepare several colors.

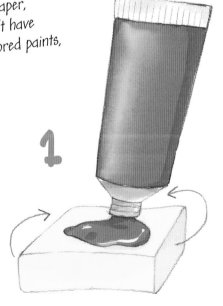

2 Fold the sponge inward as shown in the drawing to cover it with paint.

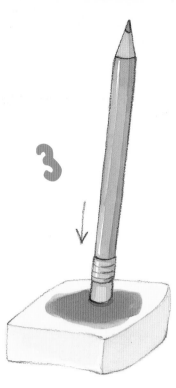

3 It's time to dip the pencil eraser either into the inkpads you bought or the sponges you made. If you make the sponges, you can choose the colors and even mix them as you like.

4 Now get stamping! You can draw freely or follow guidelines by putting the drawing under the paper and following it.

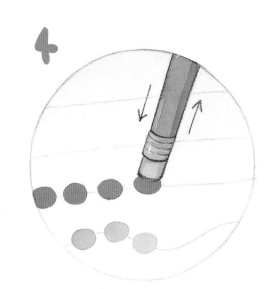

Notice that you will have to keep dipping the pencil into the colors, as they become less intense each time you stamp. And remember to clean it each time you change colors.

23

A BALLERINA

with your hand

See what a cute tutu you can make just by using your fingers.

MATERIALS: Paints and paintbrushes, a plate, cardboard, a pencil, scissors, a hole punch, glue, sticky tape, a needle and thread, necklace beads, and a ribbon.

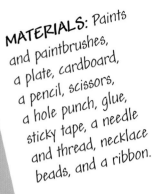

1 Squeeze the paint you want to use onto a plate. Wet the palm of your hand, pressing it down so that the paint completely covers all your fingers.

2 Spread your fingers as wide as you can and stamp your hand onto the middle of the card. Do it again, keeping the palm in the same place but moving the fingers slightly so that the stamps end up in the free spaces.

3 When the paint is dry, draw a ballerina: her body, head, and limbs... Color her in with paints.

4 Now you just have to add accessories. Make a cut on each side of her waist to put a ribbon through and tie it into a bow. Make a bead necklace: Put the thread through one side of her neck, thread several beads onto it and insert it through the other side of the neck. Tie a knot in the back and secure it with a piece of tape.

If you stick a little bow into her hair with glue, she will be even prettier! It could make a nice greeting card to give as a gift!

THE SEA with Modeling Clay

By using two basic clay modeling techniques (sausages and balls), you can make loads of printing stamps.

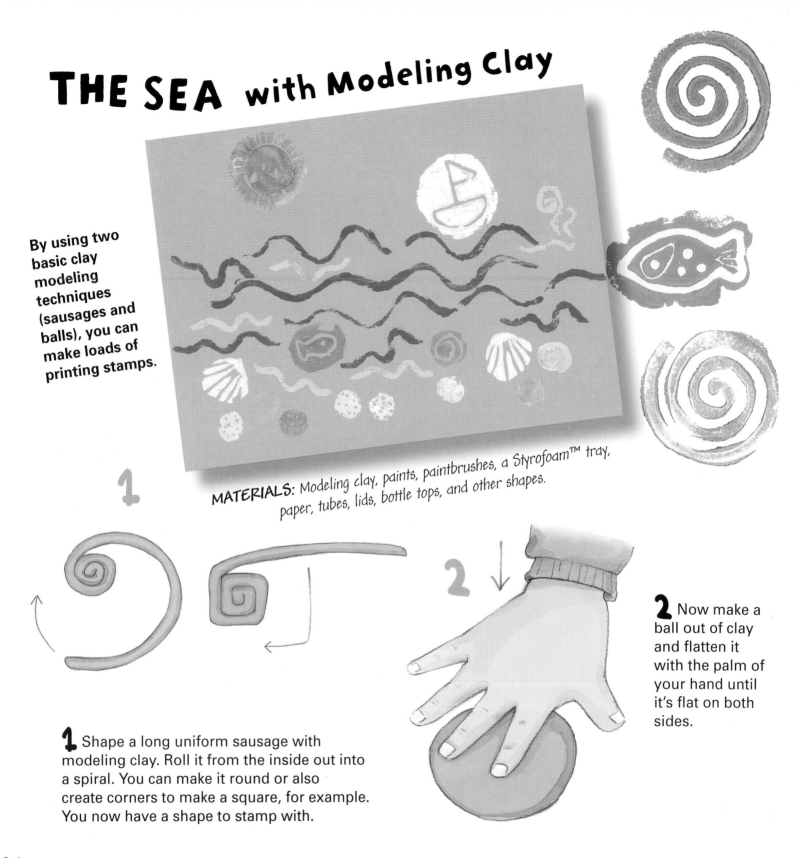

MATERIALS: Modeling clay, paints, paintbrushes, a Styrofoam™ tray, paper, tubes, lids, bottle tops, and other shapes.

1 Shape a long uniform sausage with modeling clay. Roll it from the inside out into a spiral. You can make it round or also create corners to make a square, for example. You now have a shape to stamp with.

2 Now make a ball out of clay and flatten it with the palm of your hand until it's flat on both sides.

26

3 Make a letter or a figure in the modeling clay using a paintbrush handle. The lines made in the clay will not have paint on them. You can also create shapes using tubes, lids and bottle caps... Whatever you can think of.

If you clean the paint well with a little water, you will be able to reuse the clay to model other shapes.

4 Everything is ready to start stamping! Pour the colors you want into the tray, wet the shapes and stamp them onto the paper. If you see that the stamps have too much paint on them, you can use another piece of paper to remove some of it.

27

A THOUSAND THINGS
with Styrofoam™

If you like using paints, keep the plastic paint trays from the supermarket. You'll see how many uses they have!

MATERIALS: A plastic paint tray, scissors, paper, a blunt pencil, a sponge, a roller, paints, paintbrushes, lids, bottle caps, and a spray bottle.

1 Cut the edges off the plastic tray so that you get a flat board. Draw something on the paper and transfer it onto the board by pressing lightly. Remove the paper and go over the lines by digging the pencil into them. You can also make marks with lids or other objects.

2 If you want to stamp the drawing in only one color, wet the roller with paint and roll it over the board you just prepared.

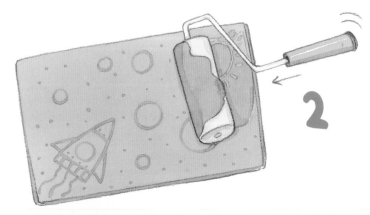

28

3 For different colored stamps, paint areas with the paintbrush. Work fast so the paint doesn't dry... Just in case, spray it with a little water from the bottle, before stamping.

4 Put a sheet of paper on top, press down everywhere and remove it. The board can be cleaned and reused many times.

If you want to stamp on fabric, for example, it's better to stamp the opposite way: By pressing the paint tray onto the surface you are decorating. Remember that fabric paint needs to be set by ironing it after the paint is dry.

29

FLOWERS
with cardboard tubes

We bet you have different sized cardboard tubes at home. Keep them and play around by combining them with this fun project we suggest.

MATERIALS: *Toilet paper tubes or similar, cardboard, scissors, plates, paints, and paper or card.*

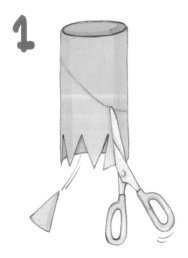

1 Cut the tube into different shapes at one end: triangles, round shapes or anything you think of.

2 Fold the shapes that you've cut outward, opening the tube wide like a flower. You can also make shapes by folding the tube without cutting it, like a heart or a leaf... Try it out!

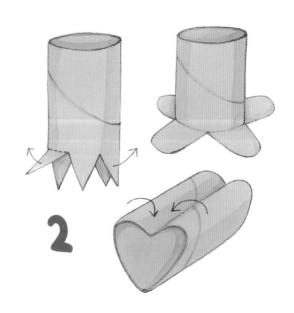

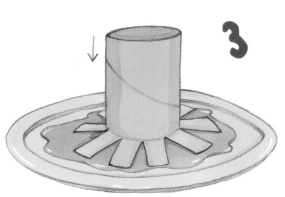

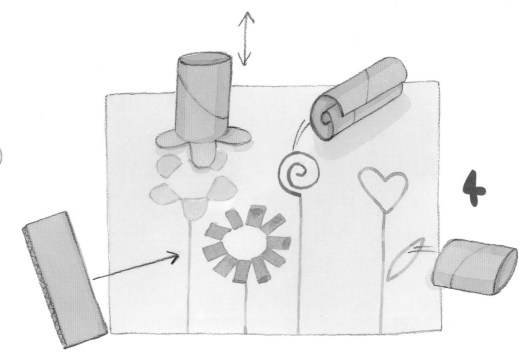

3 It's time to pour the paint onto the plates and start wetting the tubes.

4 You can use the shapes you made to stamp different types of flowers, for example. If you cut a tube from top to bottom, you can make a spiral! And you can make stalks with the edge of a piece of cardboard.

Try making a mural for your bedroom. You can celebrate the arrival of spring!

31

SEALS

from foam on cork

Sheet foam is very easy to cut, so you can use it to make a variety of shapes and make your own stamps.

MATERIALS: A sheet of EVA foam, scissors, corks and plastic lids, double-sided tape, paints and paintbrushes, a hole punch, pencil, cards, glue, and plates.

1 Draw little letters and drawings that you want to make into stamps on the foam. Remember that they have to be smaller than the stamp (you could draw around the lid first to use it as a guide). For letters that have holes, start by making the hole and then draw the letter around it. Cut it out.

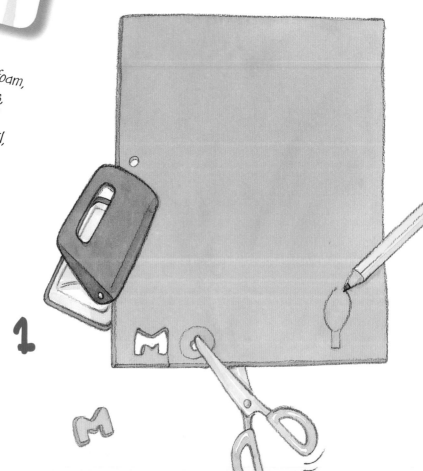

2 Stick the shapes onto the lids with double-sided tape. Be careful with the letters! Stick the tape onto the letter as you would read it: although you read it backwards, it will be right when you stamp it.

2

3

3 Pour the paint into the plates and dip the stamps you made in the paint.

4 Now get stamping on the cards or wherever you want! You can apply two colors to the stamp with a paintbrush.

4

Make the complete alphabet and you will be able to stamp words and cards as gifts.

A MANDALA with vegetables

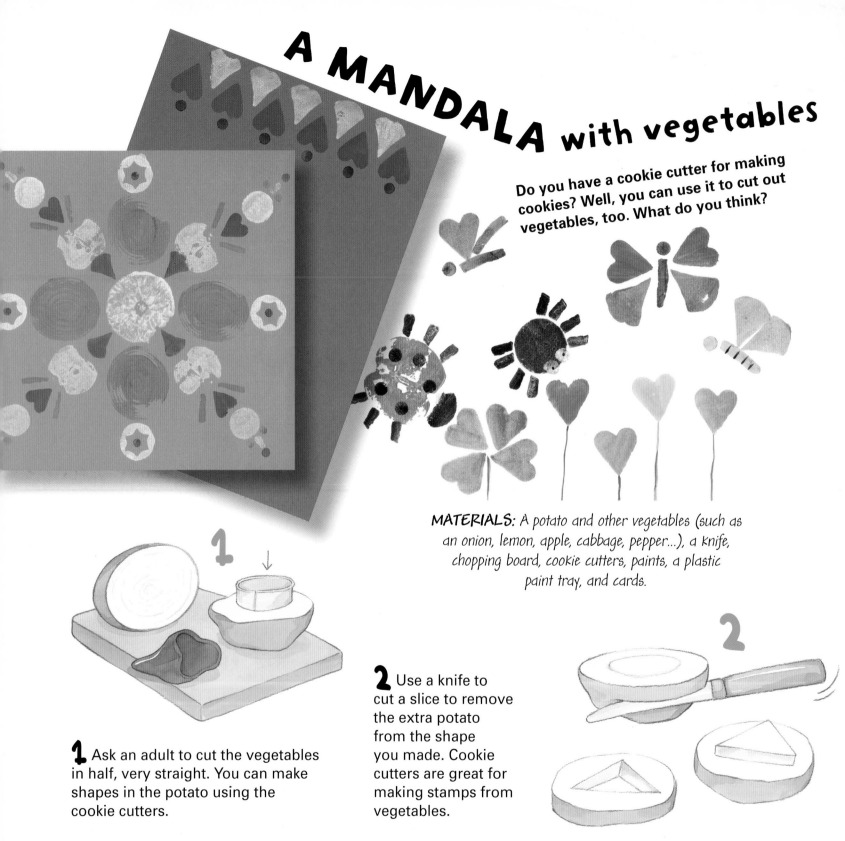

Do you have a cookie cutter for making cookies? Well, you can use it to cut out vegetables, too. What do you think?

MATERIALS: A potato and other vegetables (such as an onion, lemon, apple, cabbage, pepper...), a knife, chopping board, cookie cutters, paints, a plastic paint tray, and cards.

1 Ask an adult to cut the vegetables in half, very straight. You can make shapes in the potato using the cookie cutters.

2 Use a knife to cut a slice to remove the extra potato from the shape you made. Cookie cutters are great for making stamps from vegetables.

3 Prepare different colored paints on a paint tray. Spread them out to completely cover the surface of the vegetables.

4 Then wet them and stamp onto the paper, combining the shapes and colors however you want. You can make a mandala or borders... Experiment with different layouts!

It's always best to do some tests to see what type of shapes you end up with, before making your artwork.

RICHMOND HILL
PUBLIC LIBRARY

JUL 23 2015

CENTRAL LIBRARY
905-884-9288

First edition for North America published in 2015 by
Barron's Educational Series, Inc.
Original title of the book in Catalan: *L'art d'estampar
utilitzant coses del dia a dia*
© Copyright GEMSER PUBLICATIONS S.L., 2015
c/Castell, 38; Teià(0829) Barcelona, Spain (World Rights)
Tel: 93 540 13 53
E-mail: *info@mercedesros.com*
Website: *www.mercedesros.com*
Author and illustrator: Bernadette Cuxart

All rights reserved. No part of this publication
may be reproduced or distributed in any form
or by any means without the written permission
of the copyright owner.

ISBN: 978-1-4380-0652-9
Library of Congress Control No.: 2014949911

All inquiries should be addressed to:
Barron's Educational Series, Inc.
250 Wireless Boulevard
Hauppauge, NY 11788
www.barronseduc.com

Printed in China
9 8 7 6 5 4 3 2 1

Date of Manufacture: January 2015
Place of Manufacture: L. REX PRINTING COMPANY
    LIMITED, Dongguan City, Guangdong, China